Drums

By Julie Haydon

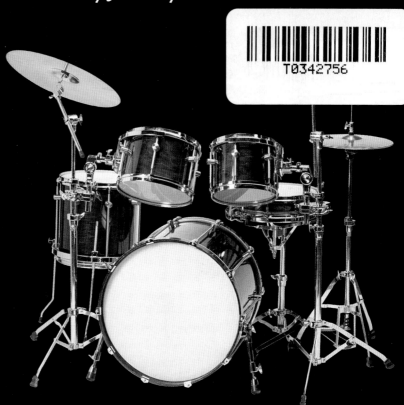

T0342756

Contents

How Drums Are Played

A drum is a musical instrument.
A person plays a drum
by hitting it with their hands,
or with sticks, brushes or beaters.

Drums can be played on their own.
But drums are often played
with other instruments, too.

A drum is a percussion instrument. Percussion instruments make a sound when they are hit, shaken or scraped.

The skin of a drum is called the head.
Drums can have one or two heads.
The head of a drum
moves up and down when it is hit.
This makes a sound.

head

head

head

The body of a drum is called the shell.
The shell is hollow.
When the head of the drum is hit,
the hollow shell makes the sound last longer.

shell

A drum kit is a set of different drums. Some drum kits
have other percussion instruments,
such as cymbals, too.

a drum kit

A drummer sits behind the drum kit to play it.
The drummer uses his hands and feet
to play the different instruments.

How to Make a Drum Kit

Goal

To make a drum kit.

Materials

You will need:

- a large tin with a lid
- a plastic ice-cream tub with a lid
- a box
- a plastic bucket
- a foil plate
- a stick
- coloured paper
- thick tape
- scissors
- two long pencils.

10

Steps

1. Decorate the tin,
   the ice-cream tub,
   the box and the bucket
   with coloured paper.

2. Put the tin, the ice-cream tub
   and the bucket
   on a table.

3. Tape up the box
to make the fourth drum.
Put it next to the tin.

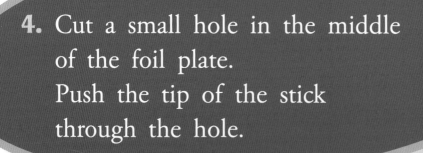

4. Cut a small hole in the middle of the foil plate.
Push the tip of the stick through the hole.

5. Tape the tip of the stick to the plate to make a cymbal.

6. Cut a small hole in the top of the box. Push the bottom of the stick through the hole.

7. Tape the stick to the box.

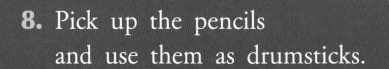

8. Pick up the pencils
and use them as drumsticks.

9. Stand behind the drum kit and play it.